I0171250

Lucky
for
Daisey

Written and Illustrated by
Lynn King Grieve

lilyboo press

Omaha, Nebraska

For Mom, who has always fueled my creativity
and been my biggest fan.

For Dad, who knew my heart.

For Mike, who loves and inspires me every day.
You helped set the fire for my first book.

Text and illustrations ©2020 Lynn King Grieve

All Rights Reserved.

No part of this book may be reproduced in any form,

printed or electronic, without the express written

permission of the publisher.

www.lilyboopress.com

Published by:

Hardcover 978-1-7346422-1-6

Paperback 978-1-7346422-2-3

Mobi 978-1-7346422-3-0

EPUB 978-1-7346422-4-7

LCCN: 2020902817

Library of Congress data on file with the publisher.

Printed in the United States of America

10 9 8 7 6 5 4 3 2 1

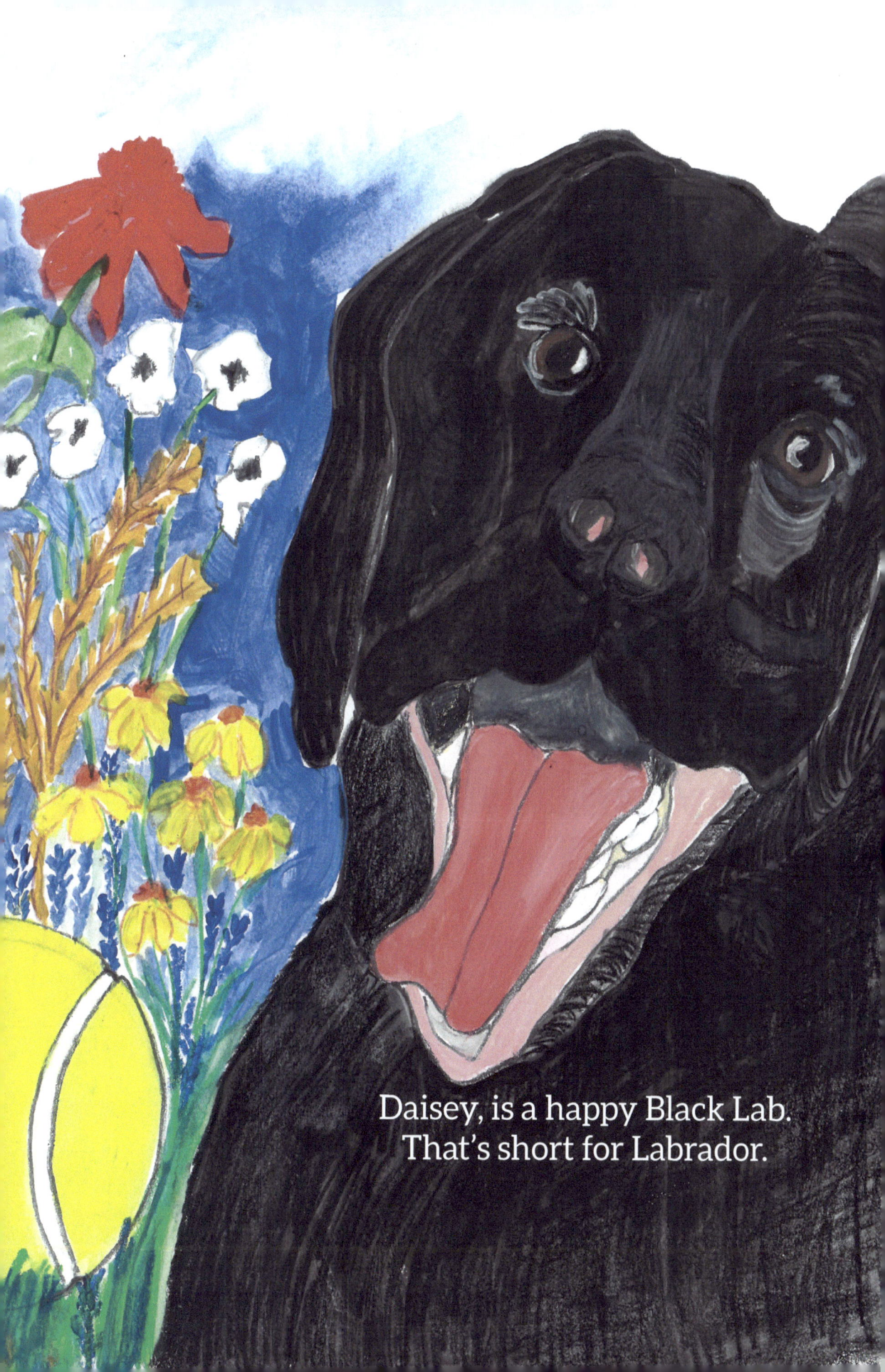

Daisey, is a happy Black Lab.
That's short for Labrador.

Daisey loves summer, which means longer days and more time to play. She enjoys breakfast in the morning as the sun is just waking up the grass.

After breakfast, Daisey jumps into her Master's big bed to take a little snooze. On some days she goes to the backyard and lays under her tree in the warm sun.

Every day, Daisey walks through the neighborhood—sometimes twice in one day! She greets everyone she meets, and makes many friends in the neighborhood. She thinks it's her job to lead Master.

Master says, "Daisey, don't pull! Who's taking who for a walk?"

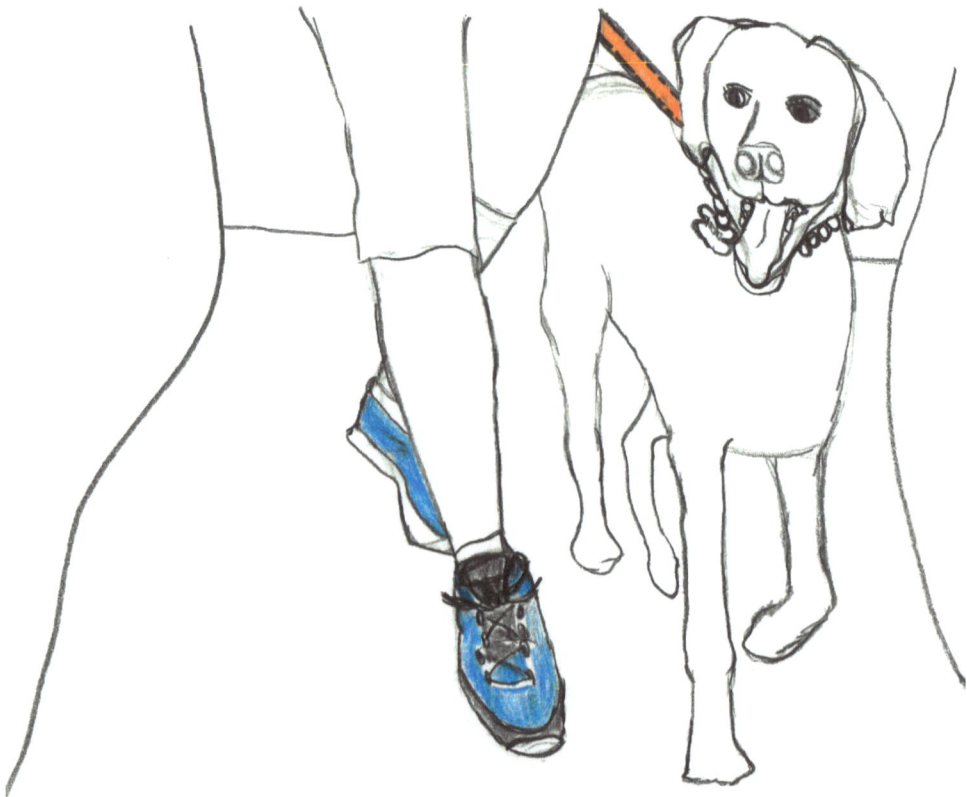

When Daisey is feeling silly, everybody around her is silly too! She is playful in an instant and can't wait to take a roll in the grass. Laying on her back and kicking up her legs is the best. She stretches, rolls, and lets her tongue hang out.

Master trains Daisey to do tricks too. She says, "Roll," and Daisey rolls. She says, "Shake," and Daisey raises her paw to shake. She says, "Dance," and Daisey stands up on two legs and shakes her butt. She says, "Smile," and Daisey gives her a big grin showing all her teeth.

Daisey's favorite game is to catch the ball and play keep-away from Master. Labs are really good at playing keep-away until they are ready for their Master to toss it again.

When Daisey is sleepy and wants to take a nap, she lays in the grass and the whole backyard seems to take a moment of rest.

Daisey listens for the sweet summer sounds of the neighborhood children playing games. Laughing, shrieking, water splashing, balls bouncing, the swishing of bike pedals, the ping of a baseball bat.

From her spot under the tree, Daisey can hear the sprinklers starting up, the birds singing, the squirrels chattering, and in the distance, the ding-ding-ding of the ice cream truck playing as it floats through the neighborhood.

The yard is her favorite kingdom. She explores every hole in the fence, every noise under the deck, every bug in the grass. Daisey likes to be right in the middle of whatever is going on.

At any moment... adventure awaits her!

Daisey hears the door and Master's bossy voice,

"Daisey, COME!"

Daisey knows that's when Master means business and all adventures must stop, and every bug in the grass has to wait.

Each time Master plants the garden, Daisey helps by digging a perfect hole for the next seeds. She knows that touching the warm ground will make new buds grow.

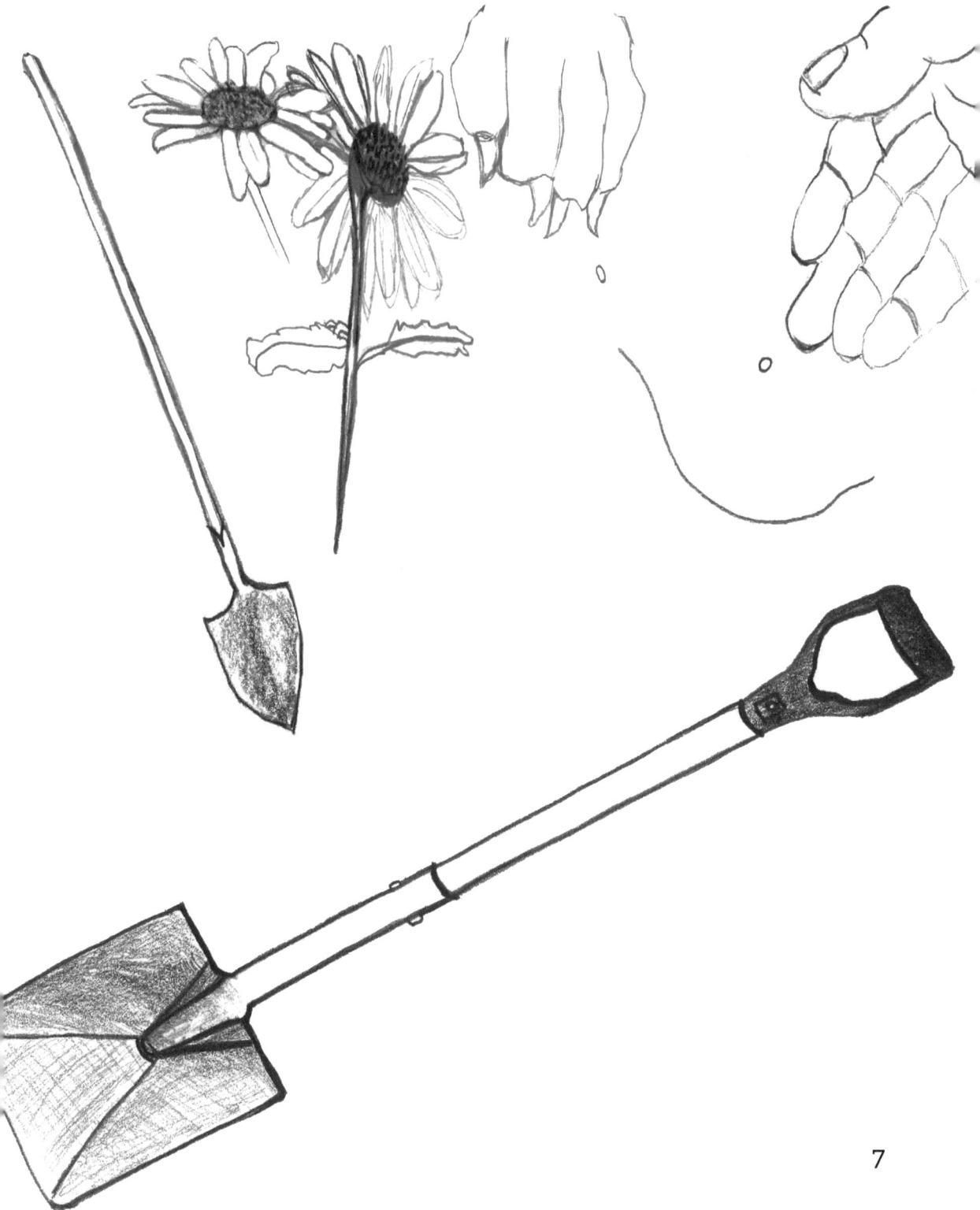

High above the yard in the trees, there is a nest with four new baby chicks and one a tiny speckled egg. This little egg is nestled into a sweet spot under his Momma among the branches, twigs, and feathers carefully arranged by his parents.

Being number 5 is pretty good. His four siblings cracked out of their shells yesterday, but Lucky got to spend another day snuggling under his Momma's belly before he came out.

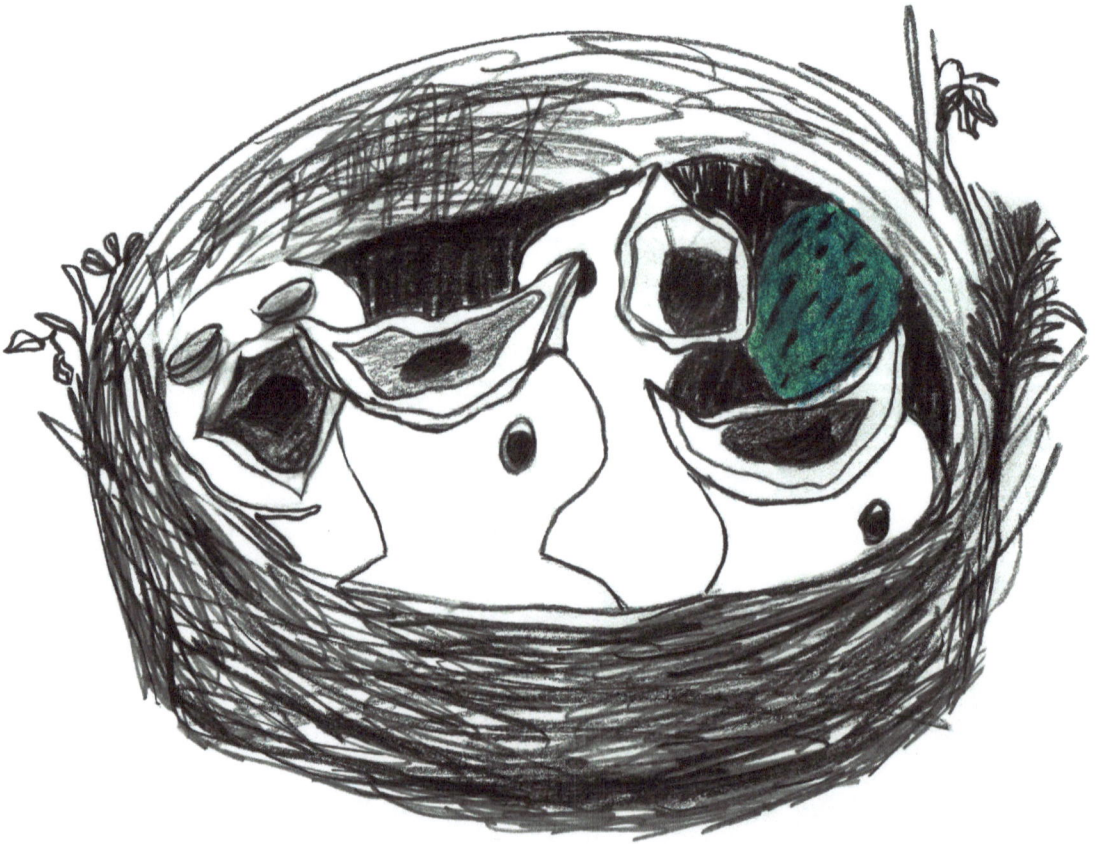

Tap. Tap. Tap. Tap.

Tap. Tap. Tap.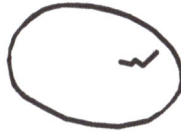

Tap. Tap.

Tap.

CRACK!

"There you are," says his Momma. "You are my perfect little bird! You took your time getting here, but one day soon you'll be big and strong. You are so Lucky."

"Yes! I am Lucky!"

Momma makes a soft spot for him among the twigs, leaves, and his siblings. He is not cold or lonely because someone is always moving close to find comfort. He feels safe because he has a comfy nook made just for him.

Not everything is easy, though.

Momma and Poppa Bird work hard to get their babies fed with fresh wiggly worms.

At feeding time, feathers fly, wings flap, legs and feet are in the air, and all beaks are open and ready for the incoming delicious worms. Somehow, the tiniest chick always ends up standing on top of Lucky's crown. Lucky is just as hungry as his nestmates, but he manages to be in pretty good position to get the best worm... sometimes.

As Momma flies to get breakfast, she chirps, "Early bird gets the worm!"

Lucky's siblings are noisy and wild, and Momma misses his beak... sometimes. He doesn't get his feathers ruffled because he believes she'll come back with more soon. Lucky's strategy doesn't always work perfectly because his Momma comes back but there are no more worms to find.

Tomorrow is another day, and every day is different.

After 13 days in the nest, Poppa Bird nudges Lucky's siblings to leap to the ground where he teaches them how to fly.

Lucky thinks he is ready, but he tells himself that staying behind might get him a juicy worm. If he is alone in the nest, then Momma will see how easy it is to feed him.

And it works.

Momma knows, as Mommas do, that Lucky needs just a little more food and a little more time. As she flies off to find those extra worms, she has a bird's-eye view of her hatchlings and she is proud. She loves all of her babies the same, but there is a good reason that Lucky stayed behind.

Lucky enjoys the gentle breeze and the extra room. It is very peaceful.

For the moment...

BOOM!

CRACK!

ROAR!

A flash of light sizzles across the sky and the sun quickly hides behind a cloud.

Lucky had seen the light show many times safely snuggled in with his family. So far Lucky and his siblings had made it through those surprises. Now he is by himself, so Lucky stays right in his spot.

The wind whips the branches, and the rain falls in hard drops that shake the nest out of the tree.

Lucky hits the ground with a thud. He opens his little beak and out comes a squawk like a giant goose! Before he discovers what his feet are there for, he tumbles crown... over breast... over tailfeathers.

Lucky skids under a large leaf and comes to a stop. He sits under the leaf to catch his breath. He closes his eyes tight and waits for the hard drops to stop pounding the ground. As the drops get softer, he opens his eyes slowly, one at a time. Right before his eyes slumbers a plump, juicy worm just for him! He snatches it right out of the ground!

The storm was loud and fast, but within minutes the air is calm again and the sun peeks out from the parting clouds.

When the drops began, Daisey ran lickety split to escape the cloudburst and find comfort in her own protected space, right next to Master.

But as the rain ends, she does not waste any time. The doggie door opens and Daisey is down the stairs and outside again.

Daisey shakes her ears—flippity, floppity, flap! She leaps over the deck and races to the fence to see what there is to see.

A good rain brings out new smells.

The dirt, grass, and air smell different, and Daisey sees the sun shining in every drop of rain.

Then she senses something new.

Suddenly she stops. There is a sound... like a happy little song.

Her keen black nose and sharp eyes drop into position to zero in on any movement on the ground. It seems so close, yet she can't locate that sweet sound that comes from somewhere—or something.

Daisey's nose examines every blade of grass, every leaf on the ground, and every puddle... until she meets a tiny, shiny set of eyes looking right back at her.

There! There it is. But what is IT?

Instantly, a crazy orchestra of sounds fills the air like confetti at a surprise party.

Daisey backs up for a second to decide what to do. Lucky, with his beak in place, is ready to push hard with his wings.

A tricky twist here, a playful jump there. Daisey, the towering black lab inches closer and closer to the "IT", and then she backs up, only to do it all over again. And again. And again.

With all of his might, Lucky takes a deep breath and thrusts out his chest to be bigger. He probably would be scared if he knew that he could be someone's dinner, just like the big juicy worm. But because he was trying so hard to be strong, he didn't realize that he was suddenly next to the black nose in full view of Daisey's brown eyes.

Lucky, the tiny bird, looks up and up and up at the big black thing and thinks, *Wow! I must be big because I'm NOT scared!*

Daisey is up for a game.

In fact, this is her favorite game—chasing and catching something. Anything.

Daisey pauses and crouches to do a staredown. Lucky sees the twinkle in her big brown eyes reflecting back at him.

Lucky stares right back at Daisey.

"I am going to catch you, you know," sighs the open mouth with the brown eyes.

"Well I am not to be caught! I know how to get where I want to go when I want to," boasts Lucky. (But he really didn't yet.)

"You do know that I could probably eat you in about two bites," Daisey says playfully.

"Well, in less than two seconds I can probably poke you with my beak. How would you like that?"

"GO AHEAD... DO IT," says Daisey.

Lucky is feeling powerful. He takes a step forward and thrusts his beak closer to her nose. Lucky just wants to put his best stuff out there.

Here was her challenge, and Daisey was all over it.

"Well... I ought to, but I... I... I'll do it when I am ready," commands Lucky. "I am not afraid of you. You think because you're bigger, you'll beat me?"

"I'm bigger and I'm faster and I have the ability to catch. And I WILL catch you... ."

Lucky raises his wings and puffs out his chest. "Do you see me? Do you see this? Do you see how big I am?"

Daisey moves back a bit and says, "Hmmmm... yes I do. And I also see that... I... can..."

SLUUUUUUURP!

Daisey wants to show this bird who is boss, but she notices his bent wing. Daisey is fast at chasing, and good at catching, but she also knows when to be gentle. Lucky for Lucky, she's good at releasing, too.

I am strong. I am big. I am strong, Lucky thinks. His heart is racing—he has never been in any danger before. In fact, this is the farthest he has ever been from the comfort of his perfect spot in the nest.

I am strong. I am big. I am strong. Lucky doesn't really believe that he is strong and getting stronger by the second, but he's trying to think so.

Lucky is learning quickly. He just knows in his heart that Daisey let go of him on purpose.

Daisey is watching and waiting for a reaction. The little creature pops back up and puffs out his chest again. Daisey is beginning to see that she likes this powerful little fuzzball.

A spark of magic touches the air.

Daisey suddenly becomes a little more relaxed, and she actually looks at Lucky and sees his strength. Lucky, the tiny bird, looks at Daisey, the gigantic lab, and sees gentleness in her eyes.

Still being careful of course, Lucky examines her by turning his head to the side to count each white tooth, the pink tongue, each tuft of fur, four legs, two blinking brown eyes, two silky, floppy ears.

Lucky adjusts his feathers again because he feels another surge of power and confidence. Lucky notices one of his wings is slower than the other and a little bent. It doesn't hurt. Lucky flutters his wings and twirls in a circle.

Somehow the giant brown eyes, enormous tail and big floppy ears do not seem scary at all. In fact, the furry black coat looks soft like Momma's feathers.

"You're ok, you know. I like how quickly you can jump to your feet," Daisey says thoughtfully.

Lucky opens his beak and sings, "I'm Lucky. Momma says I'm a big strong bird!" His sweet sounds fill the air and travel across the sky.

Daisey, who is always ready for a new friend, says, "I'm Daisey. Master tells me I'm a good dog."

Daisey suddenly remembers Master. *Where is she? Does she see what is happening here?*

Daisey sees Master standing on the deck and leaves Lucky in the grass to let Master know she found something exciting after the storm.

"Did you find a new friend, Daisey?"

Daisey's tail wags ninety miles a minute. She leaves Master and ambles across the yard to Lucky, and looks back at Master and does her best dance with a big "WOOF!" and a smile.

Lucky hadn't moved a feather. He feels safe now and he happily watches as Daisey returns. Daisey plops down right in front of him.

Lucky opens his beak and exclaims, "You're back!" Lucky is so happy he jumps up on Daisey's nose.

"Hey, how did you get here anyway, little Ninja bird?" said Daisey.

"Yep, that's me! Wait, what's a Ninja?" Lucky asks.

Daisey grins, showing all her teeth. "A Ninja is strong and fast. They are fearless and agile. They pay attention and know how to keep themselves safe. They are their own Masters."

Lucky jumps to the top of Daisey's head and sings.

"Yep, that's me! I'm quick and brave and strong, a Ninja!"

Daisey says, "Wanna see my yard?"

She runs to the fence. "Here's where I watch sneakers walk by, and wheels from strollers and I also meet other good dogs. This is my favorite spot."

Daisey takes Lucky to her pool. "This is my cool down spot. Master and the long green snake fill it to the top with water in the summer so I can splash around. It's my favorite!" Daisey leans down and dips her nose in the water. Suddenly Lucky slides down into the water, but Daisey quickly scoops him back up with her nose and right back onto her head.

Lucky shakes himself from the top of his head to the tip of his tail feathers. Drops of water spray out from his wings. "That feels SUPER!"

"Next is Master's garden. She calls it her happy place. It's my favorite. I help her dig holes to plant seeds, and then flowers grow. That's why she calls me Daisey, because I am her happy!"

"Daisey, you're my happy too," Lucky sings.

"Over here is the best place to hide my bones. I have lots of places like this, but this is my favorite."

"Daisey, you sure have a lot of favorites," Lucky squeals.

"You're right, but my favorite favorite is right under the Dogwood tree. The grass is soft and it's the perfect place to take a nap."

A sudden gust of a wind blows Lucky from the top of Daisey's head. Chink... clack.... The sound of the back gate latch releasing... and BLAM... Whomp! The gate flings open and smashes against the fence, as Daisey flips around just in time to see her best squeaky ball bounce right out of the gate and down the street.

"MY FAVORITE BALL!"

Off Daisey bolts to chase her ball leaving Lucky on the ground with his eyes wide open. Daisey moves fast!

"Daisey, how will you catch it???" cries Lucky as he leans forward to try to help her.

Wait, Lucky... wait for her to return. He waits... and he waits... just like when he's waiting for Momma to bring him a fat worm. Only it feels like his feathers are tingling and that he cannot be still.

Lucky feels the leaves and sticks swoosh by his head looking for Daisey. He sits still staring, hoping, wishing.

I have to move... I must help Daisey find her favorite ball. It looks so far, but I can't wait any longer. I know I can do it.

With all of his might, he flaps his wings until his body rises a little off the ground. It is just half of a worms length, but his tail and feet are barely off the ground!

Try again! Lucky puts one foot down and then another. He jumps up even higher and flaps his wings only to fall on his belly.

Ugh, I have to… C'mon Ninja… I need to… let's do this!
And up he goes… up and up… Lucky is flying!

No time to think… no time… go… go… go to the gate!

Lucky flies high and out of the gate he goes. He looks up and down. He goes to the light post on the corner and perches himself on the edge for a second so that he can see. To the right and then the left. Strange things are floating in the wind and tumbling down the street.

He does not see Daisey, but he knows, as friends do, that she needs him.

Lucky flies after a twirling bag and just as it dances itself into a corner, he finds Daisey huddled with her ball with her eyes hidden under her gigantic paws.

"Oh, there you are!" says Lucky. "I found you, Big Friend."

Daisey whispers, "How did you get here, Lucky?"

"I went like this

and that

and up

and up and around…

And swoosh! I can be in the air like Momma and Poppa!"

"You mean you flew here?"

"Yep, I am a Ninja who can fly! Come with me and I will take you back," says Lucky with pride.

"C'mon it's easy. Let's go"

Lucky skillfully leads the way back home because he now has a bird's eye view. He is strong and brave—he is a Ninja after all.

Daisey feels happy because she has a new favorite friend! The new buddies take a nap on the soft grass right back under their favorite dogwood tree.

It was a good day.

Every day thereafter, Daisey and Lucky help Master in her garden. They play together, splash together, and explore their favorite spots together.

Momma and Poppa Bird and all of Lucky's brothers and sisters live nearby and fill the yard with song.

Together, they all live with their happy.

www.ingramcontent.com/pod-product-compliance
Lightning Source LLC
Chambersburg PA
CBHW040033050426
42453CB00003B/103